D1762416

Barbie®

Barbie
What A Doll!

by *Barbie*
as told to Laura Jacobs

Artabras A Division of Abbeville Publishing Group
New York * London * Paris

Front cover: 1997. Satin bell-skirted gown dotted with rhinestones; shawl-collared satin evening cape.
Back cover (clockwise from top left):
    1959. Striped coat and matching sheath dress; see page 68.
    1970. Mock turtleneck with culotte pants; see page 40.
    1988. Straight skirt with blouse and jacket; see page 19.
    1998. Fitted suit with leopard-print collar and hat; see page 17.
Spine: 1993. Red faux-leather fitted mini-dress accented with silver belt and earrings.
Front flap: 1996. High-waisted mini-dress with pink velour top and yellow skirt; see page 37.
Back flap: 1997. Yellow rain slicker with coordinating hat; see page 67.
Page 2: Sleeveless white silk gown with full-gore bias-cut skirt; see page 123.

Editor, 1st ed.: Amy Handy
Editor, 2d ed.: Jeffrey Golick
Designer: Molly Shields
Production Manager: Richela Fabian

BARBIE and associated trademarks are owned by and used under license from Mattel, Inc. All Barbie doll images and art are owned by Mattel, Inc. Copyright © 1994, 1999 Mattel, Inc. All rights reserved.

Copyright © 1994, 1999 Abbeville Press. All rights reserved under international copyright conventions. No part of this book may be reproduced or utilized in any form or by any means, electronic or mechanical, including photocopying, recording, or by any information storage and retrieval system, without permission in writing from the publisher. Inquiries should be addressed to Abbeville Publishing Group, 22 Cortlandt Street, New York, NY 10007. The text of this book was set in BeLucian Book. Printed and bound in Hong Kong.

Second edition
10 9 8 7 6 5 4 3 2 1

The Library of Congress has catalogued the Abbeville Tiny Folio edition as follows:
    Barbie: four decades of fashion / introduction by Barbie as told to Laura Jacobs. — [Rev.] 2nd ed.
      p. cm.
    "A tiny folio."
    ISBN 0-7892-0461-4
    1. Barbie dolls—Clothing. I. Title.
NK4894.3.B37B38 1998
Rev. ed. of: Barbie : in fashion. 2nd ed. 1994.
688.7'221—dc21   98-8808

Artabras ISBN 0-89660-0990-8

Contents

 A Life in Fashion, by Barbie * 7

Tailored Chic * 11

 **At Ease** * 25

Trouser Styles * 39

 **The Sporting Life** * 51

 **Outer Wear** * 63

Intimate Apparel * 75

 **Career Moves** * 81

Party Girl * 93

Very Special Occasions * 111

 **For the Holidays** * 137

Appendices * 142

A Life in Fashion

by **Barbie**

as told to Laura Jacobs

I've never been really good at talking about myself. I think actions speak louder than words, and ever since I first started gaining notice as America's most famous Teenage Fashion Model I've always tried to put my best foot forward. Leafing through this book, a photo album gathering together the fabulous fashions I have worn through the years, I suddenly realize how much has happened during my lifetime. It's been a high-flying roller coaster ride, and you, my wonderful friends and fans, have enjoyed the thrills and chills with me—all the time inspiring me, confiding in me, caring for me. I couldn't have done it without you.

Today, models have become big business. Like actresses and entertainers, fashion models are superstars with incredible incomes. But when I began my modeling career in March 1959, the world was a different place. The stars were up in the sky—and in our eyes. After I answered yes to my first photo assignment, I hung up the phone and jumped for joy. When I floated back down to earth, I went straight to my desk to look up the word "model" in the dictionary.

1997
Pale plum satin suit with wide lapels and tapered
sleeves and skirt

"A miniature representation of something; an example for imitation; an ideal." That definition in *Webster's* told me almost more than I wanted to know about the career path I'd begun. Of course it was thrilling to be the first girl in high school to earn a real live paycheck—simply for wearing the most beautiful clothes in the world! But now all eyes would be watching *me*. Girls I didn't even know would look up to me. I decided I wasn't going to let them down.

Right from the start, I was known by just my first name. In fashion, this is a time-honored tradition. If a model is lucky, her name will be a perfect match for her look and character, almost symbolic. In my first decade of modeling, the 1960s, there was huge Veruschka, an endlessly exotic Russian, and skinny Twiggy, a tender British shoot. As you can see, compared to these, Barbie is a rather ordinary name. But it turns out that I was in the right place at the right time, because fashion was ready for a girl who could represent all-American can-do and enthusiasm.

There's no question that my full figure caused a sensation. Some people say I was America's answer to France's yé-yé girl, Brigitte Bardot. But I've always been more apple pie than cheesecake. In 1959, the year I debuted, the hourglass shape was the ideal, and the many minutes a girl spent on her appearance each day were considered an important part of self-image. Eyeliner, lipstick, and a powdered nose, undergarments that smoothed and shaped the body into predictable curves—these were the foundations of an ensemble. An ensemble style was the key to elegance. And elegance was the result of discipline. In 1960, all a teen had to do was look to America's First Lady, Jacqueline Kennedy, to see that only out of effort came effortlessness.

When I first began modeling, makeup was a bit more emphatic. Eyebrows were carefully sculpted, and for two years mine arched in a cool, sophisticated manner. Eyeliner, especially, required a super-calm hand (I took a deep breath before drawing each line), and for many years I preferred an almond-eyed tilt, very Sophia Loren. Suntanning was definitely *not in*, and my skin was an ivory bisque. Early in the sixties, though, my makeup artist relaxed my brows and toned down my lip and nail shades to a pale pink (a sort of strawberry ice cream), and we began highlighting the rosy tones in my complexion. In 1971, during a trip to Malibu, I got my first tan.

If you look through my portfolio, you will notice a softening of rigid rules in makeup. I see a transformation from a very exact and formal self-presentation, an almost theatrical stress on perfection, to a more informal, natural kind of beauty. When I look at my early self, I see a young woman who seems to be keeping secrets. The way I look today—smiling so much you can see my dimple!—strikes me as more direct and ready for anything.

Even my hairstyles reflect the trend toward brush-and-go preparation. Once I let my hair down in the late sixties, I never really went back to fancy coiffeurs. From the seventies on, I've worn my locks long and wavy, and have settled on blonde as the color that suits me best (though I still love to experiment). But for years I had a handful of classic colors—White Ginger, a creamy platinum, and Titian, a Renaissance auburn—and distinctive hairstyles that came to be identified with me. Many people still remember my very first "do"—that famous swing ponytail with the poodle bangs.

Some people cringe when they catch glimpses of their old selves, but I adore how a hairstyle or cosmetic color brings back the atmosphere of an era. Chocolate Bon Bon and Cupa-Co-Co are not just guilty pleasures that test my waistline, they're two of my haircolors from 1969, and they conjure up the plain-spoken sensuality that started the seventies (remember, *Hair* didn't hit Broadway until 1968). An even better form of remembrance is the touch and sight and even sound of the clothes one wore. The feel of the fabric. The character of the construction. The line, the length, the *look*. Boy, did I wear some beauties. Say "Barbie" and people will describe fashion favorites from as far back as '59, as if it were yesterday!

As I said earlier, my timing couldn't have been better. When I took my first—dare I say nervous—turn down the runway, fashion was still measured in the magical, manicured hands of this century's great international houses: Balenciaga, Chanel, Dior. It was a time of couture classicism and my early ensembles spoke with a daring French accent, and sometimes with a bit of Italian.

And yet change was in the air. Ballet dancer Rudolf Nureyev defected from the Soviet Union in 1961, the Twist untwisted decorum in '62, Valentina Tereshkova became the first woman launched into outer space in '63, and in their collarless suits, the Beatles blasted off on Ed Sullivan in 1964.

Everyone, everything was getting aired out. My beautiful ensembles of the early sixties, such a pleasure to wear, yet requiring such planning and unflinchingly perfect posture, gave way to kickier, more youthful designs. The "ensemble" as we knew it (coordinated shoes, gloves, handbag, and hat), loosened its grip on our lives. And we began to move differently. British and American designers gave us clothes that danced—the Frug, the Pony, the Mashed Potato—and I wore, or rather danced, them all. The Mod years were here.

Am I upsetting anyone if I say that the 1970s weren't my favorite decade for design? The force field fizzled, and the seventies saw a regrouping, a rethinking, a return to grassroots and groundswell. Ecology and economy were the bywords of the time and in fashion terms that meant knits, linens, wools, in league with synthetics of all kinds.

In 1980, the movie *10* (as in "a perfect 10") came out and, to my mind, set the tone of the decade. Women were ready to do and have it all. To be or not to be perfect wives, mothers, and career professionals, all at once—that was the question. The women characters on popular nighttime soap operas like "Dallas" and "Dynasty," whether they were CEOs or MRSs, glittered in glamorous gowns and power suits, examples of a new female elite. This stress on grasping and sculpting our own destinies went hand in hand with the fitness trend, which set a new standard for female strength and shape. Muscle was in, indolence was out; "definition" was *the* watchword. It wasn't just upper arms and midriff that we were redefining, but our place in society.

A curious thing happened to me in the 1990s. I became an "icon." That's a fancy word intellectuals use when they want to say something or someone is both famous and symbolic. Which is what happened to me in 1994, when I reached the thirty-fifth anniversary of my modeling career. Suddenly everyone was writing books and articles about me: remembering my debut in 1959, analyzing my figure and my fashion influence, and honoring my amazing popularity and staying power. Parties were thrown for me all around the world. It was exciting and touching. Dazzle has always been a part of my mystique, but as you can see in looking through this book, the sparkle has usually been in my step or on my dresses. Oh, on occasion I have worn a diamond or two, and in the 1980s I went with the flow and wore fun faux jewelry (I'm absolutely mad about the little green palm tree earrings that went with my polka-dot bikini in 1988). My first gold hoops are now classics, and I would hate to lose one. But of all the gems one might choose from, pearls have been my constant companion. I treasure their modesty, their mystery, their luster, their life. If I were a jewel, I like to think I would be a pearl. A pink one.

Tailored Chic

No form of clothing makes you feel as strong and secure as the tailored suit or three-piece outfit. Stepping into a pencil skirt or sheath dress or Chanel-style suit is like meeting up with your secret self—those seams, darts, armholes, and kick pleats know all about you. Because of my long, slim line I've been lucky enough to wear some of the most contour-conscious designs in fashion history.

In the 1960s my suits bore the unmistakable stamp of the Paris couturier—they were constructed to a fault and could probably hold their shape without me in them. Thick tweeds were the textile of choice, in colors from pink to maraschino red to salt-and-pepper (there is nothing more chic than a black-and-white suit), and were trimmed in luxe materials like satin and faux fur. In the 1970s and '80s I wore extremely vertical suitdresses and matching tunic-and-skirt ensembles. Through the decades, however, my hemline has been pretty constant. Except for a rare mini here and maxi there, my ideal tailored skirt length was just below the knee. As Coco Chanel once explained, "When the wind at the airport blows your skirt, it shouldn't blow too high, just enough to see the beautiful legs."

1965
Tweed sheath skirt; tweed jacket with cape sleeves and decorative buttons; matching scarf with faux-fur trim; faux-fur hat

1988
Slim white jacket and skirt trimmed with gold-and-black braid;
gold-and-black metallic top with peplum; faux-fur stole and hat

1966
Pink sheath dress with satin top and cotton hopsack skirt; matching hopsack jacket with satin trim and front tie

1965
Gold, red, and brown tweed jacket with shawl collar and cuffs edged in faux fur; matching sheath skirt and hat

1963
Black-and-white tweed suit with red knit bodysuit; matching hat

1965
Cream wool and gold lamé tweed suit with flared jacket, sheath skirt, and gold lamé top

1965
Blue linen jacket with shawl collar edged in emerald green
satin; sleeveless sheath dress; matching hat

1963
Emerald green satin suit with shawl-collared jacket and sheath skirt
with peplum flounce; sleeveless white satin blouse; matching hat

1985
Sea green knit jacket with velvet magenta collar and matching hip belt; straight pink taffeta skirt

1989
Dress with magenta crepe top and houndstooth-print miniskirt; full-cut magenta jacket; coordinating accessories

1988
Printed crepe wrap dress; brushed tricot jacket with wide lapels and cuffed sleeves; matching purse and hat

1998
Peach satin fitted suit with long-line jacket and slim skirt;
leopard-print collar and hat

1965
Red linen sheath dress trimmed in red braid; linen bolero jacket with faux-leopard-fur collar and trim

1964
Red cotton sheath skirt; sleeveless white cotton blouse with red topstitching and buttons; matching purse

1966
Red satin coat; white-and-silver lamé knit dress; white broad-brimmed hat trimmed with tulle

1988
Houndstooth-print straight skirt; diamond-plaid blouse;
red single-button brushed tricot jacket; coordinating accessories

1959
Black faille coat with gathered yoke and patch pockets;
apple-print sheath dress

1966
Red georgette tunic with matching skirt,
lined with red taffeta

1993
White knit suit with gold trim and coordinating
hat, necklace, and purse

1988
Red and white floral-print jacket with V-neck and peplum;
matching gored skirt; white scarf and hat

22

1964
Pink knit cardigan with wide collar and gold buttons;
matching knit shell; pink flannel sheath skirt

1962
Full-skirted pink floral print and polka-dot dress
with ruffled eyelet insert

1996
Suit in lavender wool with gold buttons
and chain belt

1968
Hot pink faux-fur suit with white vinyl belt;
silver knit blouse and tights

At Ease

There's a certain realm of dressing that's almost undefinable but you know it when you see it. I'm talking about outfits for shopping and lunch, a Sunday brunch, a Superbowl bash, or a sunny stroll on the boardwalk. Before denim took hold as a fashion fabric, a baby-blue passport to anywhere and everywhere that only looked better the more worn and faded it got, casual clothes required extra thought and attention. My array of sun frocks and shifts, jumpers and minidresses wear touches of fantasy that to this day conjure up social afternoons and elegant reveries. My 1960 powder-blue corduroy with the birdhouse on the skirt is a haiku of homebound happiness. Rickrack and ruffles, baskets of fruit and felt appliqués, these outfits tell their own stories: not "once upon a time," but *free time*.

1959
Blue-and-white cotton sundress

1960
Full-skirted powder-blue corduroy jumper with felt appliqué;
white cotton puffed-sleeve blouse

1972
Blue denim halter top and cotton
patchwork-print skirt

28

1966
Sleeveless A-line dress with black cotton top and
black-and-white-checked taffeta skirt; matching hat

1981
Calico-print Western-style dress with faux-suede
cuffs, belt, and vest

1981
Red-and-white calico-print blouse with Western-style yoke;
sheath-style denim midi skirt

1965
Long-waisted dress with red bodice, flared blue skirt
with white print flowers, and red bow

1966
White crepe jacket with decorative gold buttons;
pleated red tricot skirt

1966
Blue-and-red-plaid taffeta dress with dropped waist,
flared skirt, and red bow

1998
Blue corduroy bib overalls with slim-striped mock turtleneck

1988
Acid-washed waist-length denim jacket; white T-shirt; gored denim skirt with white topstitching

1988
Denim miniskirt with wide pink lace ruffle and silver studs; white cotton knit T-shirt with rolled cap sleeves

1989
Acid-washed denim cropped top with pinstriped insets and neck bow; matching miniskirt; sailor cap

1988
Denim jacket with fringed yoke and silver studs; denim silver-studded miniskirt; pink scarf

1976
Bicentennial dress with fitted blue bodice, flounced sleeves,
and red skirt printed with Revolutionary soldiers

1991
Dark pink fringed jacket with blue top and southwestern-style skirt;
cowboy hat and concha belt

1988
White nubby-knit sweater with royal blue cowl collar and cuffs; royal blue calf-length knit skirt; matching knit cap

1989
Yellow vinyl miniskirt with diamond-print sleeveless blouse

1976
Navy-and-yellow-striped wraparound tunic with navy trim and belt; solid navy A-line skirt and slacks; matching hat

1969
Lemon yellow velvet minidress; yellow nylon ruffled collar
and hem trimmed with pink, white, and gold rickrack

35

1968
Red orange minidress with purple and yellow stripes;
yellow plush faux fur cape and matching hat

1989
One-piece sleeveless yellow and white sweater dress
with short knife-pleated skirt

1968
Op-art print miniskirt and sleeveless blouse
with decorative buttons

1981
Pink romper and wraparound skirt

1967
A-line dress of yellow, green, and red polka-dot panels
trimmed with black braid; matching hat

1971
Velour purple-print peasant dress with laced bodice
and ruffled hem and cuffs

1996
High-waisted mini-dress with pink velour top
and yellow skirt

1966
Empire-waist cotton sheath dress with polka-dot bodice;
matching hat

1979
Halter-style dress with red bodice
and long floral-print skirt

Trouser Styles

Palazzo, cigarette, stovepipe, bell-bottom, ski, capri—I'm describing, of course, pants of all kinds. Each design conjures a different world, a different class, a different weather. In the 1960s, when my modeling career took flight, pants were coming into their own as a fashion statement. Courrèges was offering the sleek, space-age one-piece pantsuit—immortalized by Diana Rigg in "The Avengers"—while London's Carnaby Street beamed out billowy velvet suits with Liberace-lace collars and cuffs. Meanwhile, bell-shaped skirts over skintight satin toreador pants were a form of Hollywood chi-chi we've never quite seen since: woman as both the vase and the flower. By the 1970s, pants were not only less arty and more utilitarian, worn by women in the workplace, they took on a newly political connotation. It was early in this decade that most high schools first allowed girls to wear pants to class, and with that change in the dress code came a new freedom, a sly and significant step in the direction of equality. With the eighties and nineties came leggings and Lycra®: pants as a second skin that celebrated—what else?—our striding-into-the-future legs.

1968
Red velvet pantsuit with ruffled
white tricot blouse

1970
Red pantsuit trimmed in yellow faux fur, with gold clasps; metallic knit blouse; matching yellow faux-fur hat

1992
Retro-look pantsuit in pink, blue, and purple with matching purse and stole, accented with pink faux fur

1975
Red and turquoise tricot halter top and matching red pants; Indian-print shawl and hat

1970
Blue peasant-sleeve blouse with mock turtleneck; multicolored culotte pants; matching minidress

1971
Multicolored mod pants outfit with fringe-trimmed belt
and wristbands

1981
White satin jumpsuit trimmed in silver lamé and
silver-and-black braid; matching cowboy hat

1982
Fluffy pink sweater and pink-trimmed jeans

1988
Waist-length denim jacket with silver studs;
pink rib-knit tank top; denim jeans

1977
Pink jumpsuit with zigzag-print tunic vest;
brown belt pouch

1994
Dressy white faux-leather pantsuit with full peplum;
short swing coat with lace sleeves and lapel trim

1968
Sleeveless pink satin jumpsuit
with sheer white lace oversuit

1982
White taffeta pantsuit with glittering pink-trimmed jacket
and pink waistband

1980
White lace blouse lined in white satin, gathered at waist;
blue tricot wide-legged pants

1984
Blue one-shouldered bodysuit with matching pants;
floor-length lace bouffant skirt trimmed with white faux fur

1988
Magenta satin jacket and jumpsuit trimmed in pink braid; pink plaid lapels, collar, and waistband; pink tulle blouse

1986
Bright red brushed-fleece reversible jacket with royal blue stand-up collar and lapels; royal blue strapless jumpsuit

1985
Multicolored tunic blouse trimmed in gold braid; grape spandex pants

1997
Black jacket over striped shirt and slim-cut white trousers

1986
Leopard-print jacket; hot pink spandex top and stretch pants;
yellow sash; coordinating accessories

1986
Electric blue metallic coat; magenta sleeveless tunic;
lime green lacy spandex leggings

48

1981
Gold lamé bodysuit and matching pants;
sheer hostess skirt edged in gold

1980
Gold metallic knit jumpsuit; white taffeta evening coat
trimmed with gold ribbons

1982
Ivory polyester rib-knit sweater with cowl neck;
ivory stretch-knit tights; brown belt

1984
Off-white knit jacket trimmed in gold
with pleated gold pants and striped top

1963
Persimmon jumpsuit with gold net hostess coat

The Sporting Life

As you may remember, the very first outfit I ever modeled was a simple one-piece swimsuit. But what a whirl of associations it had: that jazzy black-and-white striping, worn with gold hoop earrings, was stylish beyond words—Chanel in Cap Ferat, Gina Lollobrigida on the Riviera, Op Art in the Museum of Modern Art. (Comforting too—the knit jersey felt fuzzy and cozy against my skin.) That striped stunner of 1959 may now be the most instantly recognizable swimsuit in history. Since then, I've worn enough swimsuits to float a Miss America contest. Well, maybe not that many—but each new fashion era saw me in a new swimsuit: Peter Max diamonds in 1966, rose tie-dye in 1970, silver lamé in 1977, a combination body/swimsuit in 1984, an itsy bitsy teeny weeny *blue* polka-dot bikini in 1988, and in the nineties, a slew of sparkly new swimsuits every year—not to mention a mermaid tail or two!

The swimsuits weren't just show, either; I've always been sports-minded. Fishing, skiing, sailing, horseback riding, and hiking have all been passions. And in the 1980s, on the wave of the aerobic workout craze, I not only wore a few sweatsuits, I even launched my own line of "Barbie 'B' Active" sportif-inspired daywear.

1959
Tailored red-and-white-checked cotton bodysuit and
"clam digger" denim jeans

1961
Short-sleeved sweater; striped cotton capri pants;
poplin car coat with toggle fasteners

1984
Pink pinstriped navy jacket with fitted waist and velvet lapels; hot pink blouse; pale pink velvet jodhpurs

1995
V-necked bodysuit in hot colors with chartreuse belt and kneepads

1984
Gray cotton knit ski suit; pink parka with white fun-fur sleeves, hood, and trim

1974
Belted orange snow suit; yellow parka trimmed with white faux fur

1959
Red sailcloth jacket trimmed with white braid;
striped cotton T-shirt; white cotton short shorts

1965
Pink-and-white-checked shorts
and pink V-neck sweater

1969
Blue cotton sailor dress with pleated skirt and raglan sleeves,
trimmed with yellow braid; yellow tie; matching hat

1965
Aqua-and-white-plaid cotton jacket; aqua boat-necked knit
blouse; aqua-and-white-houndstooth stretch capri pants

1962
Tennis dress with pleated skirt; white cotton sweater edged in red orange piping

1984
White tennis jacket and matching skirt with pink trim; pink knit bodysuit

1986
Two-tone fleece jogging suit

1986
Yellow cotton-knit tank top and matching shorts; lavender cinch belt

1964
One-piece pink swimsuit with ruffled skirt;
brunette, titian, and blonde wigs

1963
Glittering gold-striped swimsuit and head scarf; brunette
page-boy, blonde bubble-cut, and titian side-part flip wigs

1971
White swimsuit with raspberry and red dots;
matching wraparound skirt

1969
One-piece swimsuit in rose and green tricot

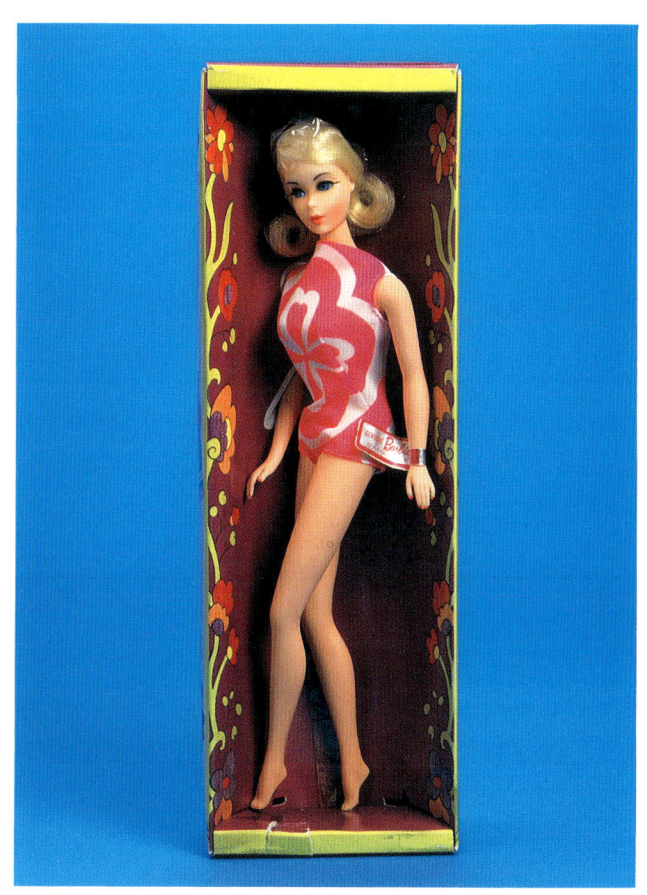

1970
Rose swimsuit with white stylized tie-dye design

1965
One-piece swimsuit with multicolored striped top
and blue bottom

1959
Black-and-white-striped swimsuit

1988
Blue-and-white polka-dot French-cut cotton bikini
with bandeau top

1994
Various swimwear in hot-colored tricot

1964
One-piece red jersey swimsuit

1989
Hot pink and black spandex
two-piece bathing suit

1995
Tropical-style bikini, black with floral print and
matching earrings

1977
White satin bodysuit with criss-cross straps,
trimmed with silver glitter

1984
Pink knit bodysuit/swimsuit with metallic trim

Outer Wear

Although most people think the color pink is my one fashion signature, there's a strong case to be made that the Barbie look has been more powerfully defined by my vast collection of up-to-the-minute coats. So many of my ensembles have included a stole, wrap, or jacket—sometimes in material matching the dress, sometimes in dramatic contrast—but always as if to say that style is like a sonnet: echoing an era, yet self-contained. What could be more slick sixties than my red "Wet Look" vinyl raincoat, more sensible seventies than my suede-look trench with faux-fur trim, more larger-than-life eighties than my oversized white fun fur, more extreme-sport nineties than my gold parka with white faux-fur collar and cuffs? If you want to wear an era, just put on the right coat. In fact, as early as 1962 I stepped out in the most unforgettable coat I have ever owned or seen, fondly known today as Red Flare. It was a Balenciaga-inspired design, a voluminous red velvet cocoon with deeply puffed and pleated three-quarter sleeves and the famous trapeze line. It was the kind of spun magic from which a butterfly emerges, and for me it symbolizes the transformational quality of the very best fashion design.

1979
Suede-look coat with faux-fur trim; tapestry-print cotton dress; twisted braid tie belt; matching hat

1979
Double-breasted camel tricot trench coat with matching belt

1979
Faux-fur cape trimmed in suedelike fabric; ribbed knit gown with high-necked gold-braid halter collar; gold braid belt

64

1969
Plush faux-fur mini-length coat and miniskirt trimmed with orange vinyl; orange mock turtleneck

1969
Brown-and-white dappled faux-fur jacket and miniskirt; hot pink satin blouse; gold lamé hip boots

1988
Bronze leather-look coat with faux-leopard lapels, cuffs, and trim;
beige blouse with matching scarf; bronze leather-look pants

1963
Red and gold lamé coat lined in red; matching sheath dress; faux-mink cuffs and headpiece

1959
Gold brocade coat lined in satin; matching strapless sheath dress; faux-mink cuffs and headpiece

1969
Orange and gold brocaded lamé dress coat with wide gold belt

1968
Striped taffeta coat highlighted with gold; matching drop-waisted striped taffeta dress with pleated skirt

1968
Metallic plaid minicoat with white nylon ruffle; matching drop-waisted minidress with nylon overskirt

1997
Yellow rain slicker with coordinating hat; plaid lining to match umbrella

1982
Midi-length yellow vinyl rain slicker; matching hat

1959
Red-and-white-striped coat with decorative gold buttons; matching sheath dress with blue skirt

1962
Full-cut red velvet coat lined in white satin; matching hat; white opera-length gloves

1967
"Wet Look" red vinyl coat with white stitching and blue taffeta lining; striped pink knit dress with red neckline trim

1970
Lamb-look fleecy white coat lined in pink nylon; matching
hat; belt, tote bag, and boots of pink vinyl trimmed with black

1986
Blue-and-white faux-fur-trimmed cape;
blue bodysuit with matching skirt

1985
Ice blue jacket and matching wraparound midi-length skirt;
faux-fur trim and hood

1988
Deep pink brushed tricot trench coat; pink and white crepe
blouse; teal linen pants; coordinating accessories

1970
Blue Mylar coat with faux-fur at collar and hem; metallic knit
minidress; thigh-high metallic blue boots

1966
Bone double-breasted leather-look coat;
matching hat and purse

1998
Navy bouclé coat with tan faux-fur cuffs and shawl collar

1997
Lavender satin suit dress with white faux-fur collar and cuffs

Intimate Apparel

Intimate apparel is just that: clothing to sleep in and dream in. Perhaps that's why my nightgowns and peignoir sets have always been in shades of pianissimo pink, sigh blue, lullaby lavender, and whisper white—fairy tale colors that are as much Sleeping Beauty as they are Krystal Carrington. In the early 1960s, when fashions required more elaborate foundations like girdles and garters (before pantyhose had come along), my repertoire of intimate apparel was a bit more various. But as feminism and fashion together moved women away from a standardized ideal of perfection and toward a more embracing acceptance of fitness and its many different physiques, we no longer needed undergarments that would shape everyone the same way. Aerobic fitness was the new girdle, and stretch fabrics like Lycra®, spandex, and jersey were used to make skirts, pants, and dresses. A figure was now akin to a fingerprint; no two bodies wore the same dress the same way.

1985
Floral print robe over
lavender nightgown

1996
Left to right: Red sheer negligée with floral bra; full-length blue voile robe;
floral lingerie with pink lace-up; blue-and-white gingham sleepwear

1982
Lace-edged robe with sheer lace sleeves over matching
nightgown with narrow ribbon straps

1986
Patterned-lace glow-in-the-dark robe with ruffled edge;
lavender satin nightgown

1984
Pastel-dotted sheer white robe with lace ruffles; white tricot empire-waisted nightgown tied with turquoise ribbon

1977
Sheer aqua dressing gown with lace-trimmed puffed sleeves and hem; aqua tricot negligee with lacy white bodice

1959
Baby Doll nightgown and panties trimmed with embroidery and satin bows

1982
Embossed silver hostess gown with silver cord trim and tie belt

Career Moves

"Solo in the Spotlight" was the name of one of my most famous dresses, a black strapless cabaret gown with a huge mermaid ruffle at the ankles that set the tone for my many forays into career dressing. From the very start I always seemed to be taking the lead and flying solo, whether it was in uniform as a Pan Am or Braniff stewardess, or as a ballerina in white tulle, or a nurse in navy cape, or as the lead in my Little Theatre Group (Guinevere and Cinderella were two of my best-remembered interpretations). From secretary to executive, model to fashion designer, dancer to rocker, I have never been afraid to try new things. In fact, in 1986 I even wore a glittering pink spacesuit with a clear bubble helmet: the sky's the limit for us women! Which is why I've made a point of playing so many different roles.

1960
Strapless glittery black sheath gown with tulle flounce;
pink chiffon scarf; black opera-length gloves

1959
Salmon sailcloth dress with white
chef's apron and hat

1985
White veterinarian's coat with pink-and-white-striped knit dress

1964
Candy-striped red-and-white cotton pinafore and white blouse; white nurse's hat

1961
White cotton nurse's uniform with dark blue poplin cape lined in red; white nurse's hat

1995
White cotton blouse under school-motif-printed black cotton dress

1967
Braniff Airlines hostess dress of pale yellow
and dark pink knit

84

1966
Pan Am stewardess suit of blue gray serge twill with fitted
white cotton blouse; matching hat

1967
Braniff Airlines hostess outfit of lavender
stretch-polyester knit

1967
Braniff Airlines "Welcome Aboard" suit
of maroon twill

85

1986
Glittery pink spacesuit with silver bodice front,
gathered sleeves, and silver belt

1967
Braniff Airlines canvas coat
with rolled cuffs and zipper

1960
Red linen suit with sheath skirt
and red-and-white-striped blouse

1992
Navy-and-white houndstooth suit with slim-fitting skirt
and yellow silk blouse

1959
Classic blue knit suit with tailored blue-and-white-checked
rayon bodyshirt; coordinating accessories

1978
Gold bodysuit, red evening pants, and flowing overskirts in
bright red, cherry red, and yellow sheers

1965
Floral-print cotton dress with green organza overlay;
shawl collar and sash of matching green organza

1964
Cinderella dress of patched burlap skirt, black cotton bodice,
and white sleeves; red bodice lacing

1964
Blue velvet Guinevere gown trimmed with floral embroidery;
gold satin-lined sleeves; blue headpiece

1976
White tulle tutu trimmed in gold braid;
white bodice

1961
Ballerina tutu of white net
over silver lamé bodice

1993
Left to right: Yellow mini-dress with purple satin jacket; purple sweat suit with matching baseball cap; black patent
leather suit with red shirt; orange hooded dropwaist jacket over chartreuse shorts and top

1998
Left to right: Orange flared-sleeved jacket with black pants; pink spangled mini-dress with sheer sleeves; chartreuse cropped T and black leggings with chartreuse side stripe

Party Girl

Who can keep count of the parties they've been to? Sometimes the best way is to remember the dress you wore, and I must say that my party clothes offer a superb history of design at its most female and fun. Some people like to say knowingly, "Barbie never wears black," but if you look at my early sixties cocktail creations you'll see ebony sheaths, capes of jet, and splashes of tuxedo taffeta—the extreme of sophistication. Shades of pink, my favorite color, have dominated my party-going wardrobe, though just one glance distinguishes a dress from the 1980s: they blink neon pink and electric blue. In 1985, I wore a line of clothing that really reflected the all-systems-go pace of the American woman: Spectacular Fashions, a multipiece color-coordinated wardrobe, offered at least four gala variations on the theme of "I could have danced all night." A sweet suite.

1989
Strapless turquoise tube dress; sheer turquoise flounce with
white polka dots; white tulle bow with center "jewel"

1966
Rose satin sheath dress with white lace overdress;
rose satin waistband with bow

1989
Pearlized lavender tricot dress with puffed sleeves
and white lace bodice

1973
Pink-and-white gingham dress with sheer sleeves
and black ribbon trim

1974
Pink-and-white dotted party dress with ruffled hem
and sheer puffed sleeves

1971
Pink satin party dress with narrow gold waistband
and handkerchief hem

1985
Dress with fitted pink lamé bodice and bouffant skirt of sheer
pink nylon floating over pink sheath underskirt

1988
Peach scented spandex minidress with six-tier ruffled skirt;
peach satin tricot stole with ruffles

1992
Pink glitter-tulle tiered skirt with silver bustier top and
coordinating metallic pink jewelry

1959
Pink dotted-swiss dress trimmed with white lace;
white petticoat with tulle ruffle and ribbon bow

1989
Fuchsia minidress with boat-neck collar; black suedelike
belt with fuchsia satin ribbon

1968
Lime green lamé bodice; pink satin skirt; pink nylon ruffles edged in lime; pink nylon minicoat edged in pink satin

1969
Pink-and-gold brocade tunic and skirt trimmed with brown faux fur and gold buttons and chains; gold mylar hip boots

1968
Sleeveless silver and blue Mylar dress trimmed in orange vinyl

1968
Minidress with turquoise bodice and yellow tricot skirt; sheer flared overskirt accented with multicolored metallic stripes

1989
Lavender tricot halter dress with silver collar and belt; detachable purple geometric-print flounce; pink tricot tights

1989
Pink tube dress with detachable pink ruffled flounce; turquoise tricot tights

1989
Yellow tunic-style one-shouldered minidress; yellow geometric-print flounce; satin cummerbund; turquoise tights

1989
Hot pink shirred bandeau top; drop-waisted skirt and stole of geometric-print sheer; white spandex tights

1990
Salmon-pink dress with pointed hem and sheer back ruffle
dotted with silver stars

1993
White satin fitted skirt and zippered blouse trimmed with gold and accented with star motif; gold cowboy boots

1988
Gold lamé dress with bodice overlaid with red lace; double-flounced
lamé skirt topped with red tulle sparkled with gold

1982
Gown with ruffled halter-style bodice and pink ribbon trim; blue tricot taffeta skirt with sheer royal blue overskirt

1965
White-and-gold diagonal-striped bodice; crepe skirt trimmed with bands of bodice fabric; white opera-length gloves

1980
Red bodysuit with gold trim and cut-out sleeves; matching wraparound disco skirt

1979
Long sheer floral-print gown with lace-edged square collar and full sleeves gathered at wrist

1985
White tricot long-sleeved blouse and harem pants; red spandex tube top

1985
Red spandex tube top; white tricot wrap skirt; red satin belt in gold-edged leaf design; white detached sleeves

1985
White tricot balloon pants; red spandex tube top; white tricot pleated wrap

1985
White tricot wrap skirt; matching blouse with deep V-neck and long shirred sleeves

1995
Deep pink ruffled short skirt with shiny pink
waistcoat-style bodice

1988
Yellow print hip-wrapped dress with gathered skirt; shiny black faux-fur boa

1964
Gold knit skirt sprinkled with glitter; matching shawl-collar blouse with V-back; black belt accented with gold

1978
Yellow satin gown with gold lamé bodice and sweetheart neckline; sequin-edged sheer overskirt

1982
Yellow gown with lace-edged flounced hem, puffed sleeves, and satin sash

1992
Mod-print long-sleeved micro-mini-dress

1959
Blue taffeta bubble dress with white polka dots;
rabbit-fur stole lined in white satin; opera-length gloves

1964
Strapless black sheath dress with black ribbon trim; sheer tulle cape

1962
Black taffeta sheath dress with cap sleeves and matching taffeta bow at neckline

1962
Black taffeta dress with flared skirt, white organdy collar, and four decorative white buttons; white organdy hat

1969
Pleated white nylon bodice; black taffeta Empire-waist midiskirt with velvet waist; sheer black nylon overskirt

Very Special Occasions

American culture has changed in so many positive ways that sometimes I feel a little guilty for wishing this, but I'll wish anyway: if only there were more chances to wear ballgowns. The floor-length formal, the gown worn to a white-tie party, is a world unto itself, with its own laws of posture and decorum, and a rustle of enchantment that makes you feel taller and more mature with every step. Each gown is different and special and I can't begin to describe the thrill of making an entrance in those magnificent sweeping skirts and sinuous columns. Then again, there were other unique creations: 1961's pale pink whip-cream swirl, 1963's seaspray formal, and 1988's mint-green ode to Saturn.

Every fashion show ends with a wedding gown, and the final gowns seen here are bridal. The white gown, of course, is our age-old image of both purity and apotheosis, the happy ending and the new beginning. I'm partial to that 1967 Dior-style gown, with its sweetheart bodice and dewy satin. It isn't merely that Olivia de Havilland had one like it. That simple tulip skirt, petals opening, is to me the perfect picture of life's eternal blossoming.

1998
Sage-green floor-length slit skirt; pink satin strapless bodice;
pink moiré jacket with deep shawl collar

1966
Ball gown with red velvet flared skirt over floor-length bouffant
skirt of white net and taffeta trimmed in red bows; opera-length gloves

1966
Ball gown with red satin bodice over pink chiffon skirt; red satin coat with rhinestone closures and faux-fur collar

1965
Red chiffon gown with ruffled hem and pink roses; white faux-fur stole lined in white satin; white opera-length gloves

1967
Strapless red taffeta dress with overskirt of sheer red chiffon edged in white maribou; red chiffon cape edged in maribou

1976
Princess-style coral slipper-satin gown with white lace inset; faux-fur stole with white nylon ties

1963
Rose taffeta ball gown accented with metallic lace; shawl-collared cranberry velveteen coat lined in rose taffeta; white opera-length gloves

1964
White satin evening gown with tulle overskirt in alternating
panels of pink and red; white opera-length gloves

116

1984
Silver stretch lamé strapless gown with bouffant fuchsia and silver overskirt; hooded fuchsia velvet evening cape

1986
Triple-pleated strapless red tube-shaped gown; silver mylar sash

1981
Red satin gown with sweetheart-style bodice and sheer tricot overskirt

1987
Ruby-red strapless masquerade ball gown with silver butterfly wings and mask

1984
Sweetheart gown with red velvet bodice; puffed sleeves and floor-length
bouffant overskirt of white sheer dotted with tiny red hearts

1989
Pink shirred gown overlaid with white tulle;
matching deep-ruffled hem

1988
Scented white spandex dress with multilayered pink circle
skirt trimmed with bows

1987
Shimmering lilac halter-style top;
floor-length pleated lilac skirt

1965
Pink satin gown with front panel printed with silver scrolls; pink tulle underskirt; pink marabou boa

1982
Fitted pink bodice accented with silver; floor-length pink skirt; sheer overskirt trimmed with faux fur; faux-fur stole

1989
Dress of pink satin and tulle printed with silver stars and trimmed with silver braid; pink boa

1994
Pink spangled sheath dress with tightly pleated pink sparkle-sheer cascade

1985
Raspberry lamé strapless fitted gown with tapered skirt and peplum waist

1985
Raspberry lamé strapless fitted bodice and tapered skirt; burgundy taffeta jacket with raspberry lamé lapels

1985
Raspberry lamé strapless gown; bouffant overskirt of red sheer patterned with raspberry lamé

1985
Poppy red tricot floor-length gown threaded with gold

1984
Red knit gown with silver lamé blouse and matching ruffled peplum; faux-fur stole; red tulle hat

1983
Fuchsia gown with sequined bodice and nylon satin ruffled skirt

1984
Magenta skirt with ruffled hem over satin spandex bodysuit; sheer boa blouse with bouffant sleeves

1976
Deep rose satin gown with fitted bodice, ecru lace trim, and flounced hem; matching sheer evening shawl

1995
Black sheath dress and opera cloak accented with gold lace pattern

1996
Sleeveless white silk gown with full-gore bias-cut skirt, accented with silver

1964
Gown with silver lamé bodice and yellow satin skirt
with silver scroll appliqué; white tulle overskirt

1988
Empire-waist scented yellow ball gown; circle skirt of yellow tulle trimmed with butterfly bows; wrist ruffles

1965
White-and-gold-striped lamé gown with gold braid straps; orange chiffon sash; white opera-length gloves

1996
Bell-skirted white and gold gown with fitted white bodice and flared peplum

1967
Long-sleeved Empire gown of white crepe with gold embroidery; gold lamé cape lined in hot pink chiffon

1988
Plum and metallic gold waist-length jacket trimmed in gold
braid; slim floor-length pleated gold tissue-lamé skirt

1985
Multicolored fitted tunic blouse edged in gold braid with royal blue full skirt

1996
Black sheath dress with paisley design and poufed red satin sleeves

1988
Drop-waisted gown with royal blue panné velvet bodice and jewel-toned metallic print skirt; royal blue hat

1992
Purple and gold lamé asymmetrical gown with diagonal pleating and one-shoulder swath

1986
White gown with glow-in-the-dark lace skirt

1963
Strapless sea green formal with fitted bodice and bouffant skirt of tulle in alternating blue and green panels over satin

1965
White lace sleeveless bodice; fuchsia taffeta and chiffon skirt; green and blue chiffon sash; white opera-length gloves

1978
Gown with green lamé halter-style bodice
and three-tiered skirt; ruffled boa

1965
Blue satin ball gown with silver lamé bodice;
blue satin cape with white faux-fur collar

1995
Faux-fur-trimmed gown with satin bodice and apricot and lavender skirt accented with silver swirls

1961
Regal pink satin gown with flowing side-draped train; faux-fur stole lined in pink satin; opera-length gloves

1979
Sheer blue voile gown with blue satin evening cape edged in silver braid

1966
Aqua satin dress; chiffon cummerbund and overskirt; faux-rabbit-fur stole lined in aqua satin; white opera-length gloves

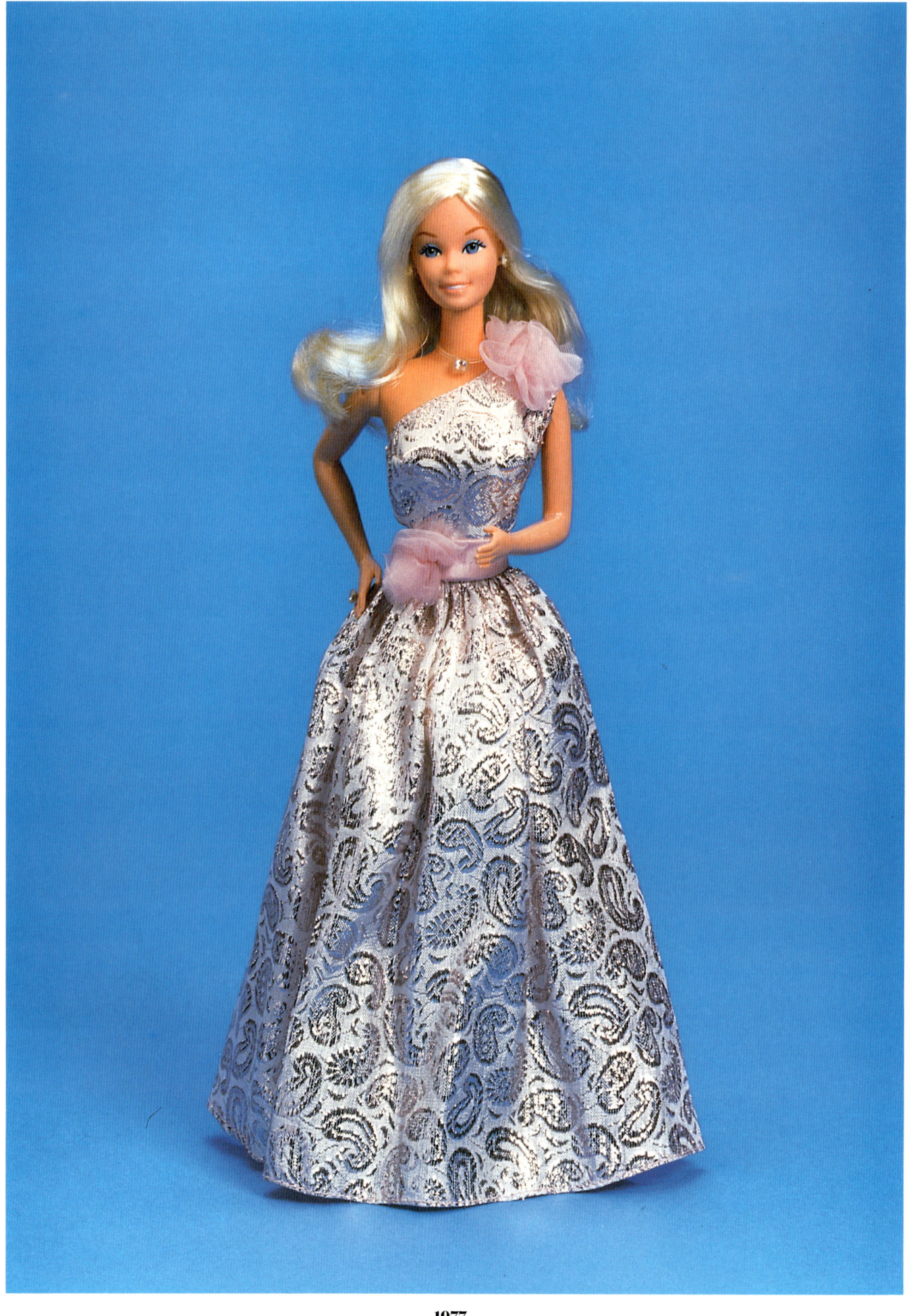

1977
Silver brocade one-shouldered evening gown
trimmed with lavender

1989
Dress of pink diamond-print metallic top with dolman sleeves;
silver lamé skirt; matching hip wrap

1959
Strapless satin wedding gown with long-sleeved floral-printed tulle overlay and three-tiered skirt

1963
Satin wedding gown with flowing chiffon overskirt and ruffled front insert; white opera-length gloves

1976
White satin wedding gown with sheer white lace tricot sleeves and train

1977
Empire-style wedding gown with lace-over-satin bodice; chiffon skirt with front panel of lace and satin

1967
Wedding gown with sweetheart bodice and flared skirt
revealing satin slip with braid trim and dotted tulle overskirt

For the Holidays

During the course of my forty-odd-year career, I've watched as the number of opportunities for getting dressed up have dwindled down to a bare minimum. When I first appeared in 1959, even an airplane ride was cause enough to dress to the nines; airports now are filled with people parading by in jeans and T-shirts. Also, in the 1990s, movie stars wear clothes from the Gap to the *Academy Awards*®, of all places.

But the holiday season remains the one time of year that continues to warrant an exceptional outfit. During this past decade I have made a special effort every December to find the perfect ensemble, one that says both "joy to the world" and "season's greetings!" As much as I enjoy change, it's reassuring and even exciting to have, every winter, a tradition to embrace.

1990
Red sparkle organza gown with layered ruffle skirt,
fitted bodice, and ruched sleeves

1991
Bell-skirted black velvet gown; bodice, leg-of-mutton sleeves, and matching purse and bow trimmed with red and white sequins

1993
Ruby-red ruffle-tiered gown with fitted bodice
and gold accents

1992
Silver lamé gown with white organza layered over skirt;
sequin-trimmed bodice

1996
Victorian-style velvet sleeved cloak over tiered gold damask
dress; white faux-fur collar, cuffs, and hat

1997
Red gown with white and gold lace; matching ribbon decorative
wings; underskirt and bodice of white chiffon and gold lace

1994
Holiday gown with metallic lace skirt and gold lamé overskirt, trimmed in
white faux fur

1995
Holiday gown with holly-print overskirt, lace underskirt,
poufed sleeves, and holly-trimmed collar

Appendices
The Barbie Family Tree

BARBIE
(b. 1959)

FAMILY

- Skipper 1964 — *(Barbie's little sister)* — Friends:
  - Ricky 1965–67
  - Skooter 1965–67
  - Fluff 1971–72
  - Tiff 1972–73
  - Ginger 1976 only
  - Scott 1980 only
  - Courtney 1989
  - Kevin 1990 *(Skipper's boyfriend)*
- Pets:
  - Honey 1983 *(pony)*
  - Butterfly 1993 *(pony)*
  - Chelsie 1993 *(pony)*

- Francie 1966–76 *(Barbie's MODern cousin)* — Friends — Casey 1967–70

- Jazzie 1989 *(Barbie's cousin)* — Friends:
  - Dude 1989
  - Chelsie 1989
  - Stacie 1989

- Tutti 1966–71 *(Todd's twin sister)* — Friends — Chris 1967–68

- Todd 1966–68, 1991 *(Tutti's twin brother)*

- Stacie 1992 *(Barbie's littlest sister)* — Friends:
  - Whitney 1994
  - Janet 1994

- Kelly 1995 *(Barbie's baby sister)* — Friends:
  - Chelsie 1996
  - Becky 1996
  - Melody 1996
  - Marissa 1998
  - Jenny 1998
  - Deirdre 1998
  - Keeya 1998

FRIENDS

- Ken 1961
- Midge 1963–67 *(Barbie's best friend)*
- Christie 1968
- Stacey 1968–70 *(Barbie's British chum)*
- P. J. 1969
- Jamie 1970–72
- Steffie 1972–73
- Kelley 1973–76
- Cara 1975–78
- Tracy 1983
- Diva, Dee Dee, and Dana 1986 *(Barbie & The Rockers)*

- Family —— Little Brother Tommy 1997
  - Friends
    - Allan 1964-65, 1991 *(Midge's boyfriend)*
    - Brad 1970-72 *(Christie's boyfriend)*
    - Curtis 1975 only *(Cara's boyfriend)*
    - Todd 1983 *(Tracy's fiancé)*
    - Derek 1986
    - Steven 1988 *(Christie's boyfriend)*
- Whitney 1987
- Miko 1987
- Bopsy, Belinda, and Becky 1988 *(Barbie & The Sensations)*
- Teresa 1988
- Midge 1988
- Kayla and Devon 1989 *(Dance Club)*
- Kira 1990 *(Wet 'N' Wild)*
- Nia 1990 *(Western Fun)*
- M. C. Hammer 1991 *(Celebrity friend)*
- Tara Lynn 1993 *(Western Stampin')*
- Kayla 1994 *(Locket Surprise)*
- Shani 1994 *(Locket Surprise)*
- Becky 1997

PETS

- Dancer 1971-72 *(horse)*
- Beauty 1980-83 *(Afghan)*
- Beauty and Pups 1982-83
- Dallas 1981 *(horse)* ┐
- Midnight 1982 *(horse)* ┤ Family
- Dixie 1984 *(baby palomino)* ┘
- Prancer 1984 *(Arabian stallion)*
- Fluff 1983 *(kitten)*
- Prince 1985 *(Poodle)*
- Blinking Beauty 1988 *(White horse)*
- Sun Runner 1990 *(horse)*
- All American 1991 *(horse)*
- Sacha 1992 *(puppy)*
- Honey 1992 *(kitten)*
- Rosebud 1992 *(horse)*
- Tag Along Wags 1993 *(puppy)*
- Stomper 1993 *(horse)*
- Puppy Ruff 1994 *(puppy)*
- Mitzi Meow 1994 *(kitty)*
- Prancing Horse 1994 *(horse)*
- Tropical Sea Horse 1995 *(horse)*
- Collie 1996 *(dog)*
- Calico 1996 *(cat)*
- Nibbles 1996 *(horse)*
- Ginger 1997 *(dog)*